THE DAY

I wanted to write a book of depressing poetry but gave up on that notion.

It's July 31, 2021, and after writing about what I needed to do in my book; _LIFE AFTER DEATH,_ my life took a turn for the worst.

Could I withdraw funds from the bank after paying my bills?

Nope

Life turned tragic for me _where I just gave up on life._ Just once, I would like to feel what it's like to have some money in the bank and be debt free. Or even, my children pay the rent for me for 3 to four months so that I could be on my feet perfectly.

I know, I know. I should not complain because millions out there are facing eviction.

Millions have and has been evicted from their homes.
Many are sleeping in tents on the roadside.

Billions are being forced to take the MARK OF THE BEAST globally. Their Covid-19 Vaccine.

If you don't take the Mark of the Beast you:
Cannot go to school
You cannot work in some sectors.

Your fundamental human rights have and has been taken from you.

You are bound in your home or apartment.

You cannot convene with friends and family as you like.

You cannot buy or sell as you please.

You cannot pay your bills
You cannot travel
You soon won't be able to get health care, and more.

Humans have and has become the slaves and prisoners for their Government and Corporate Demons; Terrorists that control it all and kill at will. Thus, the Death Toll of Covid-19. Hence, Spiritually and Physically Covid-19 is linked and affiliated with and to Death.

Therefore, the MARK OF MAN – BEAST – THEIR 666.

Therefore, humans globally truly do not know that Covid-19 is their implementation fully of the Mark of the Beast. Thus, many have and has interpreted Revelations wrong as well as, forced to get their vaccine; Mark of the Beast.

Symbolism is a distinct language. A higher language used in the Spiritual Realm that many; nations cannot decipher until now.

So, be grateful Michelle because at least you have a roof over your head and if they were to announce food shortage right now, you would in a better position than some because; you have food to last you a while.

Yes, I've started to stack up for myself and I am starting to stack up for my dad as well. I have enough rice to last me and my children for I would say a year depending on usage. We don't eat a lot of rice at home.

The guy came to spray my apartment yesterday but did not spray because; the chemicals he uses we cannot stay in the apartment neither can our dog. I was not here as he told my son, *one of the chemicals can kill us therefore, no one; not even our dog can stay in the apartment.*

Not going to worry because I need to get out of this building and fast.

At the bus stop coming back from the bank I was hearing this conversation with this young lady and her boo – boyfriend I would imagine. And I am saying wow to myself. She is actually talking to him like that.

Some women lucky to get men they can boss around. But then, I truly do not know their situation and so not interested.

I've been by myself most of my life and I have to wonder what it's like to have someone do all for you. Cater to you and make you feel as if you are on top of the world. Just listening to her tell him what she wants and what he must cook for her, and his mother cannot help him to do it is like wow. A shi wear di pants inna dat dey relationship from the way she was talking to him, and telling him what he must do; _she is one lucky Black Woman._ Shi get a weak man fi real because most Jamaican Man don't stan fi bullshit.

Listen, it's their relationship. For me, I truly do not want or need a weak man in my life. My partner have to be strong, and we have more than mutual respect for each other. Abuse is a no no but hey, he can treat me like the delicate Michelle I am on some days.

So yes, my day is shit. I can't fully and truly cannot do what I want and need to do. Oh my God plus, going back home I wanted to get breakfast. Yes, I was going to use my credit card to pay for breakfast. I just put money on it and I am still owing money on it, but because I was down and hungry, I wanted to get breakfast.

Could I get breakfast?

No. They barred off the area to walk to get to the Jamaican Restaurant. I was pissed because I had to return home without breakfast and with my back wow.

No, I am so sick and tired of the construction everywhere. I still do not know why they have to rip up the roads so much. It is totally not necessary. Areas that needed no repair they've uprooted and created so much traffic. You know what, leave it alone because; this is just their way of keeping you inside literally in my view as well as, mash up Earth. Thus, the Concrete Jungles globally.

So, I had to walk back home. Walking home extremely slow, I thought of *WALKING AWAY FROM LIFE LITERALLY.*

No, my walking away is moving out of my apartment, and leaving my kids to pay the rent fully.

What is it like to have someone pay your rent for you fully?

What is it like to not having to have to worry about paying your rent on a monthly basis?

Just that freedom where you don't have to pay for anything just for those couple of months because all is being taken care of for you. Wow

Yep, wishful thinking on my part.

Man, I have so many books in my bedroom that I need my own library. And even when I have my own library, I still would feel as if I don't have enough books. I have to add more books to my library.

Yes, today I want and need a relationship with someone.

Please forgive me here because I am going to be rude; disgusting sexually.

But:
My vagina has been closed off for so many years it need some true Vitamin S right now. Yes, as we Jamaicans would say:

"MI NEED ILE."

Yes, my inner parts need oiling people.

So yes, I am in the stage where I need to back it up
Skin it out
Follow mi mine
Tek charge
Bruk dung di bed
Feel good
Feel im stamina
Feel im breath on me

Yes, mi a goh run wey inna him
Him inna mi

Laade to mi aunda him

Knowing me, he would get bored of me because I've been out of the game sexually for so long.

Let me stop here because I am feeling the boredom of my life Sexually right now.

Yes, I am extremely picky when it comes to men.

He has to fit and meet my criteria's life wise, cleanliness wise, truly giving wise, kind wise, affectionate wise, family wise, God wise, and more good and true things. I have to fit and meet his criteria's life wise, cleanliness wise, truly giving wise, kind wise, affectionate wise, family wise, God wise, and more good and true things.

So yes, relationship wise, I am down on myself.
Financially I am down on myself.
Living wise, I am down on myself.
But apart from that I am so good to go.

I am blessed in many ways though it is a bit hard financially.

Planted my second set of seeds and I am hoping they grow good and true, sweet, ever growing positive, healing, and more good and true things like my first batch. I truly cannot wait to see the first batch budding and or sprouting soon.

There is so many things I want and need to do, and I am hoping to do them. Yes, I was down on myself this morning, but I am so much better now. It is so cold it feels like it's autumn with the breeze coming in on me.

I can't close my window because I have my seedlings on my windowsill. I'll just go under my sheet soon.

My dreams I've not talked about, and I do not know if I want to talk about them.

The Moon is on my mind right now.

Did I see the Moon showing me a speckled ripe banana with a little bit of black on the skin?

Yes, and I truly do not know what this mean. I am hoping the Moon with shine its light on my seeds and help them to grow good, true, positive, healing, ever growing, and more good and true things.

Further, did I see the face of a Male in the Moon?

Yes, but I was not sleeping. Therefore, this is a waking state vision. I am sure it was a White Man's Face I saw. So, I truly do not know if the White Race of Demons here on Earth is going to come to an abrupt end real soon.

And no, I have not started to edit my book *LIFE AFTER DEATH.* I so do not know what I am waiting on.

Right now, I need the Wisdom and Strength of God. Earth is like a disaster zone with what is happening here on Earth. Therefore, Earth must continue to cleanse herself. Humans have and has done so much injustice to her; Earth. I complain about my financial woes yet, she is going through so much at the hands of humans.

How does she cope?

How does she stay sane with the wickedness and evils of humans?

In all that is happening, I cannot have compassion for humans because humans hath no compassion for self and others.

Politicians have and has turned Earth into a War Zone; the Battlefield of Death.

Humans have and has turned Earth into a War Zone; the Battlefield of Death.

Earth is overrun by Demons.
Humans live for all that is wrong.

Humans fight for all that is wrong.
Humans believe in all that is wrong.
Humans cater to Death.

Humans have absolutely no respect for humans.

Humans have no respect for the different borders they have with each other nationally, globally, and more.

So no, I cannot worry about humans. I have to think of my life now because something is truly not right. I don't think I am getting cold as a human, but I do have to think of my life good and true. I have to secure my future and state with God. I do not know what is coming from the Sky. Something is being shielded from me. Thus, truly woe be unto man – humans.

So yes, I need to be strong because all that is happening with Covid-19 is nothing compared to what is to come in my view.

I truly do not know about the finances of the world; world economy right now because it's not good future wise. Allelujah

To what I am feeling; there is going to be a disastrous economic collapse along with the scarcity of food; wow. THIS I KNOW FOR A FACT WITHOUT DOUBT.

It's weird. When I look at life and the past of the White Race, and the atrocities they've carried out over the ages, I still have to ask why?

Babylon did do a lot of wickedness and evil things to Black People this I know, and God has and have excluded them out of life because; *not one Babylonian can be found on the Mountain of Life, nor are there any Mixed-Race Babylonians on the Mountain of Life.* I still have to wonder.

Why are the White Race of Demons not evicted off God's Mountain?

Why should they have time to destroy?

Did Babylon and her People not get evicted out of Life truthfully?

So, what makes the White Race so special Lovey that they; the White Race had 1 Spiritual Day – 24 000 Earth Years to deceive?

No Lovey, why do you allow this race to bargain with you for life here on Earth?

They cannot bargain with you in the Spiritual Realm; why here on Earth?

Why allow Whites to bargain for their life here on Earth?

No, cut their bargaining off. They; Whites should not have any bargaining chip here on Earth Lovey.

Yes, I know Death but 2032 is vast approaching therefore, let all evil be done everywhere. No exception Lovey come on now.

Lovey, we cannot base life or your life on lies, or historical lies Lovey come on now.

Humans have and has been living in lies for just about 24 000 years, and the lies must stop Lovey come on now.

The lies and evils of the White Race; any race cannot move forward Lovey come on now. Now Lovey, I am going to move forward with this. I know the White Race are not apart of life, but I need confirmation of this with the Mountain of Life. If every White Person no matter, colour, creed, gender, language, and more are officially excluded from Life let me see none on the Mountain of Life.

And everyone, before I could finish the sentence, I was being reminded of a *WORLD WITHOUT WHITE PEOPLE.*

So, despite my horrible day and evening, I have to give God thanks. My rent and bills are paid. I know for the rest of the week things will be fine for me because I know God will truly provide for me.

Walked my dog not too long ago as it's 9:27pm and she's just spread out by my chair. I have to bathe her again before it gets ridiculously cold and throw away her bedding. I need to get her a comforter. I have to see about getting her one because she is so going to need it for the winter.

I truly have to cut her nails real soon because two of them is way too long. Yes, she trusts me to cut her nails, and this is good for me and her. The absolute trust she has with me is truly more than awesome.

I am so going to do something truly different. I am so going to have a Jamaican Beer. No, I am not a drinker, and I cannot tell you the last time I had a drink. Was it on my birthday?

So can't remember but I've had these beers in my fridge for months and I am going to drink one. So not like me, but to the way my day and evening is going, I need to be rebellious in this way drink wise. Mind you, I do not like alcohol. It does alter my body, and I can't drink a bottle of beer but; tonight I am going to do my best to drink the bottle of beer. Mind you, I might get tipsy, but I am in my home; well bedroom.

So, truly do not be shocked if I drink a beer.

11

Oh God that is bitter, and I am so feeling the effects of the brew right now. My body is so not used to this. Do I want to finish this?

Wow, why did I do that?

Why?

Next time I feel like having beer, I am going to call the lots of you to join me because this is so not nice.

Now I want to giggle.

I so can't finish this.

There's almost a half bottle left, and I don't think I can finish it. Honestly, my body is truly different. So, the rest I am going to use it to wash my hair tomorrow. Just can't take the feel so, I am going to lay down for a little bit. My body is getting weak and my eyes feel sleepy so, until later and or, another day; well, tomorrow hopefully.

Michelle

Man did I ever sleep right away. So no, I am so not a drinker because alcohol affect my body negatively. Slept good though.

Back pain letting up. Still there but not to severity. Was able to walk to Walmart which is across the street from where I live. Got all I needed except for writing paper but that I will leave for another day. I am good to go on laundry needs so this is truly great. Hopefully, during the week I can get another bottle of Fleecy. Then I will be ahead on laundry needs this way.

Other than that, I am so good to go. At the rate I am feeling now, I want to start going for longer walks but I will not stress my back out.

There's so many things I hope for right now. I was thinking of people who are in warm climates that have the opportunity to plant their little garden and vegetable garden, *and I think them to be blessed.*

Life is a blessing for some however for me, I think my life is hell here on Earth on some days.

I was also thinking about the life some live and I have to ask.

HOW CAN YOU LIVE DAY IN AND DAY OUT IN HATE?

HOW CAN YOU LIVE DAY IN AND DAY OUT IN STRIFE?

I truly can't hence, I truly cannot be around confrontational people.

Why live to die?

No, I truly cannot see myself living day in and day out around people who live to hate and fight with other people.

What is your life worth when you do all this shit?

Some people teach hate; why?

What did that race, or person do to you for you to hate them?

When I look at what Germans did to many in the Black Race in Africa; I have to beg God not to save this Race of People.

No, you do not murder a Race of People due to your greed and or, what the Demons of Hell tell you to do.

In all that Demons tell you to do; they own your ass, and you have nowhere to go other than hell because; the beating you are going to get in the grave and in hell wow.

All the wrongs you do here on Earth comes at a cost; Spiritual, and Physical Death.

Thus, it's humans that extend the Life of Death.
It is humans that give Death Life.

It's humans that let the Demons of Hell feed off them.
It's humans that are the hosts for the Demons of Hell.
It's humans that are the hosts for Death literally.

It's the 1st day of August and I am okay.

Home alone with Queenie as it's almost 3pm and all my kids are gone now.

Queenie is laying beside my feet. I do not dare move the chair or it will roll on her face.

Not going to write much because I truly do not need to.

Hopefully tomorrow I can print off *LIFE AFTER DEATH* and begin editing that book. Not going to add anymore to it because I truly do not want or need to.

As the months progress I truly hope all will be right with me.

I so have nothing to do therefore, I am going back to playing my game as I do not know what to write right now.

Further, just waiting for September 22nd to come.

Have an interview on the Nikki Clarke Show for which I am looking forward to.

As for my dreams, they were of family and a male figure I know in real life. Him wanting to be with me in the dream. Meaning, he was ready to have a relationship with me. Him holding my hand, not red, but purple onions, work, and some other things that I cannot remember.

So not going to worry about these dreams as one person showed up at my door therefore, one of my dream came through.

Thinking of a relationship, *I truly do not know why men have to lie.*

15

Why do I always get the ones I truly do not want in life?

IS IT THAT HARD TO FIND A CLEAN PARTNER THAT FITS YOUR NEEDS AND OR, CRITERIAS OF NO CHEATING, TRUTH, CLEANLINESS, PROGRESSIVE THINKING, THE RIGHT EVERYTHING?

Yes, I am extremely picky, but this is truly me.

You know what; maybe I should learn to make my own robot to suit my specific needs only for me.

Queenie is gone into the living room. She has the entire run of the apartment.

Yep, she's drinking her water. She is staying in the living room because I cannot hear her coming back to my room.

Wow, my day-by-day actions. Before I know it, you are going to know everything about me. This is great but wow.

Gone to play my game.

Later guys.

Nope I can hear Queenie coming. Yep, here she comes.

Nope she is so not staying away from me for long.

So need to try and have some fun because my life is so damned boring it's not funny. But what do I do for excitement?

Let me leave things alone because mi boring from birth.

16

It's 8:55pm and you would figure the area would be lit with parties; well people having fun, but it isn't. It's starting to drizzle outside, and my son is home from his jet skiing adventure, now he's going to the Keg for dinner.

I am so happy for him because he's having a bit of fun for the summer. You can't travel and the ban is somewhat lifted to do things and now he's doing it. This is so good for him because it's good to have fun in your life.

Hopefully by next year I can have some fun on my own. Yes, I have to be fully and totally debt free back pain wise.

Lutan Fyah – BACK IN THOSE DAYS

It's unfortunate....no, we cannot relive the past. Life move(s) forward therefore, you have to move forward in life. Absolutely nothing can stay the same. Changes do occur; must occur.

When you look back in the past; was life truly peaceful?

People still hated each other thus, the evils humans do unto each other. Yes, it would be blessed and good to live in true peace here on Earth *but for Evil, you cannot live in true peace or peace.*

Evil hath a job to do and evil is doing their job. Therefore, Death cannot be tamed or caged here on Earth. The damage is already done therefore, *LIFE CANNOT PROGRESS IN A POSITIVE WAY.*

DEMONS RUN EARTH THUS, THE DIFFERENT ELECTED LEADERS THAT OVERSEE THE DIFFERENT COUNTRIES;

NATIONS GLOBALLY. DEATH IS THE AGENDA FOR EVERY POLITICAL LEADER HENCE; HUMANS ARE LIKE UNTO CAGED ANIMALS.

Humans are truly not free to go and come.

Borders are set up.

Some humans are diabolical in that they love conflict; therefore, they truly love control, and it matters not how they control you; as long as they have people behind them to push their evil agenda.

Evil Beings that are not afraid to kill you for their POLITICAL SLAVE MASTERS AND OWNERS, DRUG SLAVE MASTERS AND OWNERS, RELIGIOUS SLAVE MASTERS AND OWNERS, PHARMACEUTICAL SLAVE MASTERS AND OWNERS, AND MORE.

Humans are truly not allowed to think freely. If humans stopped to think, and look into things they will find the truth, but for the masses this cannot be. Humans cannot think freely because they will know the truth and walk away from the lies they've been caged in, under, around, and more.

Thus, the Merciless hath no Mercy for humans.

Michelle

18

Is my last child getting on my nerves with is attitude?

Yes

But I have to learn to ignore him because with him, he's confused in life in my view. It's his way at times or no way at all. Conversation Wise at times when it comes to his views and beliefs; he is Linar. To him, he's always right, and I cannot take this in him.

But besides that, I sent out my first tweet in over 3 years of not being on Twitter. Man, has the platform changed!! I feel like an alien.

Yes, I only did one tweet. I am going to do a couple more tweets and then leave it at that. I am treading on foreign territory that I truly do not like.

I will try to write a couple inspirational tweets to send out but other than that, I want to retreat in my own little world and bubble of freedom; well, freedom my way.

And yes, I am so bored of YouTube because there is absolutely nothing on that Platform for me, Movie Wise and Music Wise.

Need to truly finish off **LIFE AFTER DEATH** *and this book, and take a well needed break from writing.*

Right now, I am disappointed in my dream world.

How can you give spiritually and not receive physically?

I am trying to figure this out.

Damn. I'm sorry.

Yes, I want a relationship and spoke about it and the Man I got holding me dream wise was truly not what I wanted. He was not Black but White.

He wasn't bad looking but frame wise with frame being body, he was truly not for me. Plus, he was not tall. He was around my height if not a tad taller than me. Body wise he was fit meaning he was not fat nor was he skinny. He was also a tad bald.

Picky yes am I, but; really to my dream world and the bullshit I am getting right now. No, please do not associate him with the bullshit I am getting. Yes, I was disappointed but at least he held me; was concerned about my back issues though he said not a word.

You know what, I should not complain. I do not receive Physically. I only receive Spiritually. Yes, I would truly like to receive Physically in goodness and in truth, but this; receiving Spiritually and not Physically stumps me.

I don't comprehend it.

People talk about manifesting things and receiving their manifestation in the Physical; here and now, but for me, my manifestation is only in the Spiritual and for me that sucks in a way.

I want and need to be held in the Physical not just in the Spiritual.

I am also at a loss because, White Men surrounds me Spiritually. Meaning, they are extremely protective of me in the Spiritual Realm.

Weird for me hey.

Yes, there's a lot that I truly do not know Spiritually when it comes to White Males and me, <u>and why they are so overprotective of me in the Spiritual Realm.</u>

Therefore, it's odd that I cannot have a good and true relationship with anyone Physically.

And to be honest, <u>I know the Spiritual Realm do not want me dating Black Men.</u> It's not a racist thing given what I've written in the different books under the Michelle Jean Line of Books.

You know what, let me leave things alone because my world is truly not your world or my world. My world is extremely harder, complex, different in so many ways, and more.

Then after getting my Man Spiritually, I received this Marijuana Plant, but it wasn't a Marijuana Plant. It was, and it wasn't so I truly do not know what to do Plant Wise.

It seems disappointment is going to be all around me. So yes, this morning and this afternoon, I am truly disappointed in my Spiritual World and Dreams.

So yes, these couple of days my life suck.

Michelle
August 2, 2021

21

Yeah, I showered, washed my hair and body with the left-over beer from Saturday. Left some of the beer in my hair and braided my hair.

Yeah me. Now I am hungry as heck. Have not had anything to eat since I had breakfast at almost 11:30 this morning. So going to get something to eat before I pass out because my sugar level is so dropping.

So, let me go make something to eat before I pass out.

Michelle

Oh man life truly sucks on some days especially when life taunts you.

I cannot go into Jamaica due to cleanliness and trust me, the negative forces around me will not let me forget that I cannot go into Jamaica with the way in which it; the negative forces around me taunt me.

I do not know about you, but Jamaica has a special smell for me. I do not know if all Jamaicans can smell this smell when they return home, but I can.

I am a country girl and the country smell different for me. It's a beautiful smell that I cannot describe and for the past two days, _I've been smelling this smell._ Therefore, I am being taunted when it comes to Jamaica.

Jamaica is special for me and the fact that I cannot return to the land due to God deeming the land unclean truly hurt me. I cannot fathom why when God give us all that is beautiful _and as Black People, we turn around and destroy it._

We allow wicked and people to come into our land and destroy land and people.

The different people in parliament in Jamaica truly do not care about the land or people because in all they do; _THEY RAPE; MORE THAN CATEGORICALLY RAPE THE LAND AND PEOPLE OF THEIR RIGHT AND RIGHTS TO LIFE._

Many steal the money of the country for their own personal gain here on Earth.

23

Some of the citizens are no better because; *GANGS ARE PREVELENT ON THE ISLAND AND MANY PEOPLE THEY KILL FOR MONEY.*

THEY DON'T CARE IF JAMAICA IS CLEAN OR NOT. AS LONG AS THEY GET PAID TO DESTROY THEIR LAND AND PEOPLE; THEY DON'T GIVE A F; BLEEP.

So no, I cannot worry about Black People because no matter our complaint we truly do not look into self, *and see that we are the ones to be destroying self; each other.*

We pay for death. There are no, ands, ifs, or buts about this. No, where is the self worth and worth when it comes to the Black Race?

All want to be someone else without knowing; you cannot be anyone else but you. Your debts here on Earth you truly have to pay for when your spirit shed the flesh.

Many live to kill because; *DEATH IS THEIR GOD YET, WHEN THEIR ASS GET TO THE GRAVE MANY ARE BAWLING LIKE A BITCH BOUT DEM SITUATION.*

BADMAN NUH CRY.

TAKE YOUR BURNING IN HELL BECAUSE YOU DID NOT THINK OF YOUR LIFE IN THE

PHYSICAL WHEN YOU WERE FLASING BOUT UNNU DIS AN UNNU DAT.

Man, many of you truly do not know your hell in hell. Therefore, I truly cannot worry about Black People because many are like wolves in sheep clothing. Dyam lie an red yie.

So yes, there are days when I am taunted by the smell of Jamaica. Thus, it's a bummer because when I smell this smell, I think of the food, the way I would get breakfast, my ease of life, going to the market, planting, walking, and just relaxing without a care in the world because all is being done for me food wise.

Man, just going to the river to wash my clothes and bathe wow.

I just can't comprehend why we as Black People continually let people influence us so negatively that we give up our life here on Earth without knowing it.

We as Black People have so much potential *but destroy all the good* we have to become; used, abused, hath no land; Earth Worth, God Worth, Spiritual Worth, People Worth, Family Worth, Self Worth, and more.

When are we going to learn to appreciate who we are?

Where we came from?
Our Black God?
Our Black Hair?
Our Black Skin?
Our Black Self, and more?

Why are we raping self of all our worth just to halla lacka fools?

Wow, let me not think of Jamaica, her people, and the consequences of the peoples' actions. A pity many truly do not know what they are going to have to face in hell when their spirit shed the flesh.

Oh Lord have mercy.

You know my mind is a bitch nigger as well. Trust me, I have to find a way to turn the chatter off when it comes to my mind.

It is hard to connect to your higher self; spiritual self when your mind chatters so much. I know the connection to my higher self via my belly button and doing certain exercises, but my mind is making it extremely difficult for me to do so; connect to my higher self.

My mind chatters a lot.

So yes, I am progressing nicely this way.

I have to get back to doing more stretching exercises as my back pain is not as severe as it used to be. Yes, I am a bit sore, but I need to be more consistent with my stretching exercises.

I need to find staying power period.

Hey, I sent out some inspirational tweets this morning. Yes, I know they went into lala land but I sent some out.

And yes, I am going to give you my Twitter feed.

My twitter feed on Twitter is:

26

MICHELLEJEAN77

I do not know if Twitter is case sensitive, but you have my Twitter feed. Mind you, I do not know how long I am going to stay on Twitter for because, *I am one to disappear after a while.* Nor do I stay long on Twitter.

I do not know if I am going to start commenting on stuff. I truly don't think I want to spontaneously. But, if you like something I post, feel free to comment, and re-tweet.

Listen, if there is a way for me to enjoy you, and you to enjoy me on Twitter via my words and your words, *we will find a way I guess.* I say I guess because; Twitter is so alien to me right now. I have to learn things all over again so truly bare with me while I adjust to this platform all over again.

Drop me a line if you can. Listen, I have to figure out DM's if there is still such a thing on Twitter. And don't laugh. I've stated in some of my other books, I am like unto a dinosaur. I like to stay in the shadows and write. If I could write 24/7 7 days a week I would. And from the way I write it might just seem this way.

I have no one to help me write nor do I have an editor to edit these books. It's just me alone baby thus, the many mistakes you will find in these books.

So yes, I am slowly coming out of my shell. Yes, I would have liked to be on a different platform to enjoy you but unfortunately it isn't this way. Hopefully, I can find the right people to design a platform for us that is independent of the norm where we can meet without restrictions and the hatred of some.

Listen, I need to be established because I know there is a better way in life. The problem is are those others that seek control.

Those that have to spread hate. I do not know why these people do not think of their Spiritual Well Being.

Do they think with all the hate they spread they're going to get away with it?

No, let me ask you this from one of my much earlier books.

"WHAT DID MY SKIN DO TO YOU FOR YOU TO HATE BLACK PEOPLE SO?"

No, come on now. Did my skin come off my flesh and come up to you and say; Joe, Denise, Frank, Sky, Braun, Richard, Carlos, Carol, Sinclair, Bev, I hate you because you look different?'

No, don't laugh. So, why do we as people hate based on Skin Tone, Hair Type, Eye Colour, Sexual Orientation? *NORMAL SEXUAL ORIENTATION* because; some are just out there sexually. And no, I will not get into this because like I said in another book; *HUMANS WILL ALWAYS SEEK TO JUSTIFY WRONGS; THEIR WRONGS.*

Life here on Earth is not about truth anymore. Life here on Earth is about lies. Thus, no one sees beyond the flesh here on Earth.

No one sees their Spiritual Future.
No one sees their Spiritual Life, and Spiritual Death.

Lies cannot justify the truth, and the truth cannot justify lies.

There's a cool breeze coming through my bedroom window, and I truly love it. While many in the world is being displaced and living in turmoil due to fire, volcanoes erupting, flood, death, heat, I was happy being cooled down by the wind; Mother Earth and her true blessings.

Honestly, I am comfortable weather wise therefore, I truly have nothing to worry about because I am well protected in this way.

Hey, what are the days in which life sucks for you?

How often do you have bad days?

Do you have someone to talk to?

Do you go out drinking with the boys or girls?

Do you get drunk?
If you get drunk; why?

And, I am so going to stop this line of questioning because my last child just annoyed me, and to him I annoy him. From his attitude, it seems as if I stress him out.

What I want and need for me to do for me is so not his way. But man, I can't wait for the day when I can live on my own debt free, and without my children.

Trust me, I am going to celebrate with God and say Lovey; what took you so long in allowing me to gain my freedom from my kids.

I truly cannot take the attitude, but this is my life, and I am so going to leave it alone because better must come and will come shortly for me.

I have to keep praying.
I have to keep trying to connect to me.
I have to keep holding on.
I have to think of my happiness.
I have to think of my life the good and true way.

I cannot let my last child piss me off because he does have an attitude problem in that he is controlling and think everyone should submit to his views, and I refuse to let this happen.

There is a better way in life, and I have to live that better way. I cannot let my children or others control me and my thinking.

I know what true peace feels like and trust me; I need to attain this true peace because it is more than beautiful.

You know, if everyone would stop and truly look at life the right way, a lot of the mess that is happening here on Earth would not take place.

True peace can be attained but you have some that truly do not want true peace here on Earth because, *they truly do not know how to live with self and others.*

Yes, I have sucky days, but man, wow.

Aye, I am so not going to let my last child get me down because; my life is truly worth it, and I truly cannot live with his attitude anymore.

I need my own space where I am free. Trust me, you will know about it because I will shout it to the Universe, and tell the Universe, Lovey, Mother Earth, the Moon, all my good and true guides to light up the sky and world in a beautiful yellow rose and let it lightly drizzle on you so that you can feel my joy and happiness to how free and truly peaceful I am.

Michelle
August 3, 2021

Reflect.

Yes, Andrew I am thinking about you. You introduced me to **REFLECT.**

It's a new day for me and I have to think. With all I see and know, why am I not more successful?

Is it the dinosaur in me?

Or

Is it just me?

Me wanting and needing to stay in the shadows as I write and write.

Me not wanting to be known personally or facially.
Me not wanting to socialize with people in that way.

Me just wanting like minded people that I communicate with my way.

What is it about life that I crave solitude?
Crave alone time
Aloneness
The Waters of Life
My Space
World

True peace is attainable
But how many want or need true peace?

Why is it that those who have no worth in life have to create war and strife here on Earth?

Why is it that these evil beings aren't swooped up in tornadoes daily and taken to the planet of Doom and Gloom as I call it; never to ever return to Earth?

Why is that people cannot see life?
Understand, overstand, and comprehend life.

What is it about life that is so wrong for the heathens that live amongst the good and true, and truly trying?

When I look at life, I have to wonder why humans take their life and self worth from them?

I have to wonder; why people do not see the goodness and truth in life?

But then; those who hath not life cannot see the goodness and truth in life because; they've got no life's worth, self worth, good spiritual growth, any kind of growth, goodness, and truth in them.

Yet, I still have to wonder; why Good was left to live amongst evil?

But then, I should not think this way because; _THE SPIRITUAL IS TRULY NOT THE PHYSICAL HENCE, THE DIFFERENCE BETWEEN THE TWO._ Yet, in knowing this, I truly do not feel better.

I have to think, reflect.
Think again
Reflect more

I see and know yet, cannot control meaning; change life for the better good for the good and true and truly trying to be good.

I want and need to plant yet, I cannot plant because I am stuck; caged in a land that I more than categorically do not want or need to be in. It's like, I am being forced to accept a land that I will forever ever have no good and true will in, or for.

Yes, life sucks for me on some days.

Right now for me, Spiritual Life sucks.
Spiritual Life cages.
Spiritual Life is poop.
Yes, Shit

But this is me on this day when I want things done right away.

I am so impatient when it comes to good and true growth.

No, don't get me wrong. Certain things I want and need done right away.

I know for me.
I know me.

Therefore, I am one that likes things done right away. Meaning, when I plant a seed, that seed should grow right away. It should not take days, months, weeks, years. That seed should begin to catch and sprout out of the Earth by the next day and not later than the next day.

Yes, it's wow and crazy for me, but this is me and the way I feel. So yes, I have to learn more about Energy, Growth, Time, not so much speed, but Speed I have to learn about too.

No, there is no serum for growth just truth, but can we fully be truthful here on Earth?

Do we not live in lies daily?
Do we not tell lies?

Are some of us not born in lies?

What about your thinking; thoughts?

What is freedom to you?

Are we truly free here on Earth?

No, I don't want to think anymore because I am truly hungry.

Need food in a major way.
Body not draining but, the hunger is truly not good for me.

Walked Queenie already and she's beside me.

Dreamt her daughter and I so hope my son do not bring her back. So cannot handle that.

Dreamt me, my sister, and dead grandmother was going through the airport. Not a lot of people was in the airport, and I had to pass though this small opening. I was telling someone about back in the day how we used to dress up in our Sunday best when we were travelling and or, going to the airport.

In the dream I was so fat too with a creamy floral dress on.

My grandmother did not walk with me though. She was walking with my sister, and they were walking fast.

I am so not going to worry about seeing my dead family members. Seeing and or, dreaming about so much of my dead family members also represent birth. I so do not know who is pregnant and or, going to have a baby real soon. I

35

truly do not talk to or keep in contact with my family like that.

Man, I am lazy now.

Breakfast for two anyone?

So need to get the hell out of Canada where I can be on some remote island just enjoying the sun.

Michelle
August 4, 2021

Come with me
Join me
Coffee or tea for two

Breakfast, lunch and dinner
Just you and me

Don't spoil the mood
The mood is right
You and me on a beach
Seychelles
No not the Maldives
You find the right place
Not too far
Close enough
Just right

It's beach time
Just me and you
Walking naked hand in hand

Please, I hope you don't mind the curves and way
Rolly Polly for some

Hey, I'm a big girl
Mampie for some
Yes, Jamaican talk
Lingo

Wait, I didn't even ask where you are from?
Jamaica
Russia
France
Belarus
Ukraine
Dominica

Grenadines
Trinidad and Tobago
Guyana

Do tell
Are you exotic
Are your features wild

Are you buff
Built like a Mack Truck

What do you look like?

No, I will see you when I get there
Meet you there

Me
No wild thoughts of me
I am simple
Plain
Ordinary

Well Plain and Ordinary for me

I can be fun
Yes, boring too

Oh well, enough about me
What about you
What excites you

No, don't answer that
When we meet, I will see
Know
Feel
Maybe touch

Do be true
Not fake
Superficial

Just be you
Truly honest
True

Michelle

The likes of men are different
Some like the big girl
Some like the skinny jean

What do you prefer?

Why does size matter?

Does size matter for you?

What makes a girl attractive for you and to you?

What turns you on when you look at a girl?

Are you fat conscious?
Do you dislike the fat or big girl?

What is it about a big or fat girl that you do not like?

Is it your status?
What people think of you?
Will think of you?

Yes, different strokes for different folks.

But what makes the big girl unattractive for you?

What makes a big girl not dateable for you?

Yes, our prejudgement.
Likes
Dislikes

The way our brain is shaped
Warped by others
Thought by others
Controlled by others

Thus, hate is truly real.

Michelle
August 4, 2021

I cannot be anyone but me.
I cannot change me to please you.

I cannot live for you because no one can live for each other.

In life, I have to truly love me and accept me for who, and what I am.

You don't have to like me. Likeness is not forced upon anyone. No, that's a lie. People are forced to like people that they don't like. Thus, Racism for some. Those who hide behind Labels, and create labels so that people are forced to like them.

Like I said, I don't have to like you. And yes, you truly don't have to like me. As long as I am not harming you, creating strife with you, and you not creating strife with me, I am good to go.

I refuse to throw labels around or belong to any group.

Labels and groups do not define me. I define me. Therefore, I have to live with me.

Listen, there are heartless people out there thus, cold blooded killers; murderers who do not care who they kill. Thus, hate is pushed by many psychopaths in this world. And like fools, you have many idiots that follow behind these weak and heartless demons. Demons who have and has taken your life's worth, self worth, spiritual worth, and more from you.

Therefore, I refuse to seek belong because; *I KNOW I ALREADY BELONG THEREFORE, I AM LIVING AND LIVING RIGHT.*

It is a fool that seeks to belong. You already belong hence your parents had you. No one can justify your life for you. You of yourself is the only one that can justify your life, add self worth; value to your life, live your life, be the good and true you in life.

Absolutely no one can tell me; this Black Woman she does not belong because; *I KNOW I BELONG BECAUSE; IT WAS MY BLACK GOD THAT CREATED IT ALL. YES, GAVE BIRTH TO LIFE INCLUDING, THIS PLANET WE CALL EARTH.*

When I can say, you get the hell off the Planet of my Birth, Ancestral Birth, the Birth of My Black God, no other nation can say this, or can lay claim to this Earth due to Black Mother; our Mother Earth.

BLACK MOTHER PRAY by Tarrus Riley feat. Jimmy Riley

Black Mothers will always pray because many of us know the truth and value of good and true prayer.

Many of us as Black Mothers can feel a higher calling; our Black God.

Many of us as Black Mothers can heal, see the past, present, and future.

Many of us as Black Mothers have the strength of God around them.

Thus, many Black Mothers know the Universe.
The callings of life.
Life

Death
More.

So, no, I cannot seek to belong when I already know I belong.

And no, Black Mothers need not go on their knees and pray because; we know the value of truth; TRUE BLACK KNOWLEDGE.

And on this note, I am so going to make breakfast.

Michelle
August 4, 2021

It's another day; a new day and I am pissed. It's 8:27am and these assholes are outside making noise with a tree shredder. And to be truly blunt and honest to the way I am pissed at these F's cutting down the trees.

There is absolutely nothing wrong with the trees and these F's are cutting them down. I can comprehend and overstand if the trees were dead; hath no life and you cut them down, but do not cut them down when they are so young, and with vibrant leaves on them.

Yes, I know it's not my property, but I do hope they are charged swiftly under the Tree Law.

I don't care if you have not uprooted the roots, you are to be charged for Tree Endangerment.

No people. I am a avid tree lover. Well, more than tree lover thus, my vengeance is going to come out when I say; *"I TRULY HOPE MOTHER NATURE; MOTHER EARTH HATH NO MERCY ON HUMANS IN DESTROYING THEM; HUMANS BY TAKING AWAY HER GOODNESS FROM BITCHES LIKE THEM; THOSE WHO CARE NOT FOR HER; WELL, OUR BABIES; THE TREES."*

No people; **HUMANS TAKE AND CANNOT REPLACE.**

THE TREE LAW IS:

"IF YOU CUT DOWN ONE TREE, YOU ARE TO REPLACE THAT 1 TREE WITH 2."

Therefore, humans disgust me to the point where I have no mercy or sympathy for any when Mother Earth; Nature retaliates, and take it all from them.

Humans have and has destroyed Earth because in full truth; *HUMANS ARE BLEEPING NASTY; UNCLEAN. And many wonder why God isn't on Earth amongst us. Therefore, it's the nasty and unclean that run Earth; oversee the lives of humans here on Earth.*

No, these assholes outside is getting to me now man. Leave the trees alone, they are not bothering anyone but no, F's like these cannot see this. They destroy; live to destroy hence they slaughter life; the life of trees here on Earth.

Scums like these truly do not need to be on Earth. Trust me, if I could, I would lock their ass out of all life and let them suffer. No, to my vengeance; I would make it so hot for them here on Earth that not even the air could help them to how hot I would make their home, car, life hot and unbearable.

No, what has the Trees of Life done to humans for humans to continually cut them down and not replacing what they have cut down.

No, if there was a portal that I could access and just dump all the Scums of the Earth in, and dump them on a planet with no water, and trees I would.

No, feel what it is like to take away the Trees of Life.
Feel what it's like to not replace truthfully.
Feel what it's like to die your way.
Yes, certain things anger me.

It angers me how Corporate Greed can get away with murder,
destroying planet Earth, destroying the Waterways of Life,
destroying; killing humans, destroying; killing the inhabitants of
the Waterways, and more.

F. I am getting super pissed at those Tree Killers outside. Man, if I could command the trees they've cut down to haunt their ass right now including in their sleep I would. Trust me, I would ensure they do not forget about the Trees of Life they've murdered.

What the F do humans think. Is it just them that hath life?

No, you take life from trees, the rest of the trees here on Earth should boycott humans. No, they should. If I were the trees I would say, "*F EVERY HUMAN EXCEPT FOR THE GOOD AND TRUE AND JUST LAY DORMANT WHERE NO WIND FLOW THROUGH AND FROM THEM, NOT EVEN FILTERING THE AIR I WOULD DO.*"

Not even food should wicked and evil humans have from any tree
to how I am pissed.

Trust me, not even the rain I would cause to fall.

Humans need to respect all life. BC destroyers.

Yes, my temper is flaring because of those worse than scums and degenerate outside. Tree Killers.

47

No, to my anger, Mother Earth should leave Canada because of those assholes outside. The trees are not bothering you, leave them alone to thrive and strive come on now.

No Lovey, and Mother Earth, I am more than mad, pissed, and angry. Look at some lands that are barren of trees. All you see are concrete jungles.

No Lovey, I truly don't like humans on this day, and I will not petition You or Mother Earth for humans. Not even the separation of Good and Evil I will petition you for because in all honest humans are truly not good.

Humans are truly not deserving of any form of life here on Earth or in the Spiritual Realm.

It's time we as humans get a dose of our own medicine. No Lovey, I want to cry for those trees.

F humans right now man come on now.

No Lovey and Mother Earth. Why the F do you have White People around just to be racist?

Why the hell can't you Lovey and Mother Earth open a portal and evict them all from Planet Earth more than infinitely and indefinitely more than forever ever without end?

We truly don't need them here on Earth because all they do is destroy and take away the beauty of Earth; you Mother Earth and Lovey to become as ugly and worthless as them; humans.

All who don't belong evict their asses off Planet Earth; from in you Mama. Mother Earth.

48

Right now, and forgive me Lovey and Mother Earth, but right now, I wish my words in all of these books were like a bullet of a gun. Yes, sting, and do damage as well as, sentence all the guilty of life here on Earth and in the Spiritual Realm to their hell in Hell.

Lovey and Mother Earth forgive me, but it bleeping hurts to hear that shit of machine going and the crap of the tree cutter going.

No, it's bad enough you have that asshole at nights with his car and loud ass muffler disturbing the peace of my nights with their bullshit to have *MORNING MURDERERS TAKING THE LIFE OF OUR BABIES.*

No Lovey and Mother Earth, how would they feel if someone and forgive me here; take them and their children and family members and shred them up without a care in the world.

No, you cannot replace their life. Therefore, no one can replace the LIFE OF THE TREE THEY'VE TAKEN.

Yes, penance is there; hence, THE LAWS OF LIFE FOR TREES. Laws humans blatantly disobey, care not for, adhere to, and more. So no, no mercy for humans.

Thus, "*HUMANS LACK RESPECT.*"

"HATH NO RESPECT FOR ANY FORM OF LIFE PERIOD."

So, Lovey and Mother Earth, I am crying out for justice for the trees that these Tree Murderers willingly and knowingly murder in the name of their so-called Landscaping. Absolutely no forgiveness for them in my book and I would hope you Lovey and Mother Earth adhere to the NO FORGIVENESS RULE; WELL, MY ASKING.

Humans need to respect life.

We can't just do all that is evil and think it's okay come on now.

Humans did condemn you Mother Earth come on now.
Humans have and has taken so much of your life from you.

Look how we've begun to plant in the name of greed – money.

No Mother Earth, take you away from humans and what will they have left?

Many will cry fowl, wickedness and evil, yet; none is seeing the evils; atrocities we as humans are doing to you Mama; Mother Earth.

It's all about humans.
Living as human.
Lying to self and others.
Dying
Killing
All that is evil.
Well, I am fed up of humans.

No Mama. Humans cannot respect you, then truly take you away from humans. Let's see how far humans will get.

No, Lovey, let it not rain for 7 Earth days Globally and truly increase the heat of Earth and see what humans would do.

Yes, many will die, but is that death due to you or me?

Is that death not due to humans and their lack of respect and true respect for Mother Earth?

Why have mercy and goodness for the heartless?

Why think of the heartless and merciless?

No Lovey, look at how some Corporate Greed dump all manner of chemicals in the waterways of life. Yes, I am thinking specifically of Jamaica now. And those degenerate of Demons in the Jamaican Government; yes, the hogs and swines that run Jamaica care not for the land. They could care less if the different corporations of the globe come in and rape the land and people of their valuables.

As long as their pocketbooks are lined who the hell cares?

No Lovey, life is truly not fair.

We talk about Africa for Africans but F that bullshit. Black People are not different from White People. We kill each other like jokes.

Are brainwashed to live in lies and do live in lies.

We are so brainwashed that we truly do not know who and what we are.

No Lovey, Black Lands are still being robbed and we as Black People cannot see this. Hence, we fight to belong in societies that truly do not like us or care about us.

We sell out Black Lands to the highest bidder to become further slaves to systems that truly oppress and kill us.

No Lovey and Mother Earth. **Why the hell do WE AS BLACKS, NO NOT WE, BECAUSE I REFUSE TO BE INCLUDED IN SOCIETIES; WORLD THAT TRULY DO NOT LIKE ME, CARE FOR ME, RESPECT ME, TREAT ME FAIR, AND MORE.**

I CANNOT BE LIKE THE REST OF DI BATTY FALLARAH'S DEM; YES, BLACK BATTY FALLARAH'S THAT OTHER RACES CAN BRAINWASH AND TAKE FROM LIFE.

Thus, MANY BLACKS AND THEIR LAND HATH NO VALUE OR SELF WORTH BECAUSE; YOU HAVE BLACK DEMONS SUCKING THE LIFE OUT OF THEM; THE PEOPLE AND LAND.

Blacks have and has become so stupid; brainwashed to accept all that is wrong; evil that they cannot see what is happening in their own land.

IF YOU DO NOT PROTECT THE WATERWAYS IN YOUR LAND, HOW ARE YOU GOING TO HAVE CLEAN DRINKING WATER?

HOW ARE YOU GOING TO LIVE?
HOW ARE YOU GOING TO EAT?

IF YOU DON'T PROTECT THE LAND IN YOUR LAND, HOW ARE YOU GOING TO EAT; FARM?

WILL YOU NOT EVENTUALLY DIE IF YOU HAVE NO LAND SPACE TO PLANT.

WHY DESTROY YOUR LAND BY ALLOWING FOREIGNERS TO DESTROY YOU?

CORPORATE AND HUMAN GREED CANNOT SAVE YOUR LIFE, OR GIVE YOU LIFE.

THE MORE PEOPLE YOU HAVE IN YOUR LAND AS WELL AS, COMING INTO YOUR LAND, IS THE MORE TAXING IT IS ON YOU THE PEOPLE AND THE LAND.

All of you do not realize that:

WHEN YOU ALLOW PEOPLE; SINNERS TO COME INTO YOUR LAND, YOU THE PEOPLE AND THAT LAND IS TAKING

53

ON EVERY SIN THAT PERSON HAS ON THEIR SIN RECORD. THEREFORE, CONSENTING TO TAKE ON THEIR SINS.

Therefore, if persons XYZ has unnumberable amount of sins on their Sin Record, you the people of that land including your land has and have added their unnumberable amount of Sin and Sins to your Sin Record.

No, don't go there. How many tourists come into your land for sex?

How many come into your land with their religious lies?
Their so-called bibles and religious books they give you.

How many adopt your children and use them; your children in their dirty little games?

Evil did spread and the lies of evil did spread with evil.

Think, but then; MANY BLACK LEADERS ARE CORPORATE OWNED AS WELL AS, OWNED BY THE GOVERNMENTS OF THE DIFFERENT LANDS BECAUSE BLACK LEADERS HATH NO BALLS, GUTS, OR SAY TO STAND UP AND FIGHT FOR THEIR LAND AND PEOPLE.

SELL OUTS ARE THEY, HENCE MANY ARE OWNED BY THE DEVIL; SATAN HIMSELF.

So yes, no wonder God deemed Jamaica unclean because; the people there in Jamaica hath no worth, self worth, value thus, FEMALE DEATH OWN THE LOTS OF THEM. Thus, Jamaica and Jamaicans cannot escape their judgement BECAUSE; THEIR DEBT TO DEATH CANNOT BE REPAID BECAUSE, JAMAICANS MADE IT SO.

So no, I have no true heart for humans given what we have and has become Lovey and Mother Earth.

Humans hath no value hence, billions will not be saved, and this is due to us as humans. Billions of humans did give up their life and self worth to become swines; the hogs, and pigs of demons literally.

Think Black People and not be foolish anymore.

Whites will claim Africa again.
Whites will slaughter more in Africa Again.

SEE WHAT IS GOING ON AROUND YOU. THEREFORE, OPEN YOUR EYES TO THE TRUTH. STOP BEING FOOLED PERIOD.

White Lands are being destroyed and Black Lands will be taken again. Therefore, it is wise and true to have leaders that value you, your land, your life, your Black God, your moral values, oversee and guide you right and true; good.

It's time we stop killing each other and start respecting each other.

The more we know the full and true truth, *is the better it is for us as a Race and People.*

The more we know the full and true truth, is the better it is for us because; *WE WILL FINALLY BEGIN TO TRULY UNIFY.*

ONCE WE ARE TRULY UNIFIED THE DEVIL AND THEIR PEOPLE CANNOT STOP US. WE CAN AND WILL STOP THEM, BUT THEY WILL NEVER EVER DEFEAT US EVER AGAIN IF WE TRULY UNIFY.

WITH TRUE UNIFICATION, WE BECOME KNOWLEDEABLE.

WITH TRUE UNIFICATION, WE WILL KNOW THE TRUTH.

SEE THE TRUTH.
LIVE BY THE TRUTH.

ATTAIN GOOD AND TRUE LIFE; GOD.

WHEN WE ATTAIN POWER GOOD AND TRUE, WE WILL BEGIN TO CREATE TRUTHFULLY AGAIN.

We as Black People can attain power here on Earth. It is us as a people who do not want or need this power.

When we as Black People attain power, we can change things.

We will become unstoppable.

Right now, we are feared because our enemies do not want us to attain life, nor do they want us to truly unify, or get in contact with the power we have within ourself. Thus, as Blacks, we have forgotten what we can truly do here on Earth.

Trust me, when we as Black People find the truth. Accept the truth of self.

57

Accept the truth of us as a race and people.
Begin to know ourself.
<u>*Unify truthfully.*</u>

<u>MOTHER EARTH WILL BEGIN TO EXPAND FOR US AGAIN, AND MORE.</u>

It's time we stop breaking ourselves up in tribes to please those who hate us, including, please those Blacks who have nothing better to do than live wrong, see Blacks be continually divided in tribes, and more.

It's time we realize our self worth.
It's time we realize our Own Black God.

It's time we as Black People begin to live good and true again.

Lands are being flooded out.
Lands are burning.

<u>BLACK PEOPLE IN BLACK LANDS, START PLANTING FOOD ORGANICALLY AND FORGO THE CHEMICALS.</u>

<u>ADDING CHEMICALS TO YOUR FOOD CONTRIBUTE TO THE DECAY; KILLING OF LIFE</u> AND YOU DON'T WANT TO BE HELD ACCOUNTALBE FOR DEATH; MURDER. TRUST ME ON THAT BECAUSE, HELL IS TRULY NOT PRETTY FIRE WISE OR OTHERWISE.

START BECOMING THE DOMINANT FORCE IN AGRICULTURE.

UTILIZE WHATEVER FARMLAND YOU HAVE LEFT AND BE VIABLE GLOBALLY IN THIS WAY BECAUSE PEOPLE ARE GOING TO NEED FOOD.

STARVATION WILL BE UPON EARTH GLOBALY.

SO, GET AHEAD FOOD WISE.

THINK
THINK WISE
BE WISER
BE SMARTER

OUTSMART YOUR ENEMIES.

PROTECT YOUR OWN; BLACK LANDS FROM GLOBAL PREDATORS.

As Blacks, we can no longer sit on the sidelines and wait for handouts. God *gave us enough land to be self reliant and self sufficient.*

We can no longer want what our enemies have.

We have to want and need Black; what God has and have given us.

We can no longer be preys for those who rob us.
Steal our land.
Come with violence and brute force.
Come in the name of religion — their lying gods.
We are better than this.

Value you.
Have some dignity and self worth.

Michelle
August 5, 2021

Evil will go to any lengths to kill. Thus, evil hath no life here on Earth nor do evil hath a Spiritual Life.

Evil is Death therefore, Evil hath no Physical or Spiritual Life.

Because evil is death, evil is Physical and Spiritual Death.

Therefore, no one can escape their death if their name is written in the Book of Death.

I've told you in other books:

"DEATH PROTECTS LIFE. THEREFORE, DEATH ENSURES NO ONE THAT IS NOT OF LIFE CAN OR WILL REACH THE ABODE AND OR, KINGDOM OF GOD."

And don't you dare say Michelle you are lying.

I will repeat.

"DEATH PROTECTS LIFE. THEREFORE, DEATH ENSURES NO ONE THAT IS NOT OF LIFE CAN OR WILL REACH THE ABODE AND OR, KINGDOM OF GOD."

And don't come with me with Jesus died for our sins therefore, we are safe and saved with God.

Now let me ask you this: *ARE YOU SURE JESUS DIED FOR YOU?*

ARE YOU SURE JESUS EVEN EXISTED?

CAN YOU PROVE WITHOUT A SHADOW OF A DOUBT THAT JESUS EXISTED HERE ON EARTH AS WELL AS, JESUS IS IN THE DOMAIN AND OR, KINGDOM OF GOD?

ARE YOU SURE YOUR NAME IS IN THE BOOK OF LIFE?

ARE YOU SURE YOUR SINS ARE FORGIVEN?

Throw this book and carry on and let the book slap you with the truth.

ONE MAN CANNOT DIE TO SAVE ALL OF HUMANITY BECAUSE ALL OF HUMANITY TRULY DO NOT BELONG TO GOD.

NOT ALL HUMANS HAVE THE SAME GOD.

DIFFERENT CULTURES HAVE DIFFERENT GODS THUS, THE DIFFERENT GODS OF HUMANS. SO NOW TELL ME; HOW CAN JESUS DIE TO SAVE ALL?

Further; DEATH AND THE DEMONS OF HELL WOULD NEVER EVER ALLOW 1 HUMAN TO DIE FOR ALL OF HUMANITY AND THE LOTS OF YOU GO FREE.

DEATH AND LIFE HAVE TO; MUST ABIDE BY THE LAWS OF LIFE AND DEATH.

LIFE CANNOT INTERFERE WITH DEATH IN THAT WAY. *And I will not explain because* SPIRITUALLY LIFE CANNOT GO INTO HELL TO RETRIEVE ANYONE.

ALL LIFE THAT BELONGS TO GOD MUST CHANGE AND GO UP TO SEE GOD.

ALL LIFE THAT BELONGS TO DEATH MUST ACCEPT THEIR JUDGEMENT; PUNISHMENT IN THE GRAVE AND GO DIRECTLY TO HELL TO PAY OFF THEIR DEBT; SINS BEFORE THEY FINALLY DIE.

Therefore, there is a Spiritual and Physical Life, and there is a Physical and Spiritual Death.

Listen, I've told you in other books:

GOD CANNOT BOW DOWN TO DEATH.

IF GOD SACRIFICED JESUS TO DEATH, THEN GOD WOULD HAVE BEEN A BITCH NIGGER.

63

GOD WOULD HAVE BOWED DOWN TO DEATH AND GOD; THE TRUE AND LIVING GOD CANNOT BOW DOWN TO DEATH.

GOD DID NOT CREATE DEATH, IT IS US AS HUMANS THAT CREATED DEATH WITH OUR SINS.

WHEN WE SIN WE CHOOSE TO DIE.

WHEN WE LIE TO OTHERS, WE CHOOSE TO SIN AND DIE.

WHEN WE DECEIVE OTHERS, WE CHOOSE TO SIN AND DIE.

WHEN WE ACCEPT THE LIES OF OTHERS; POLITICAL LIES, RELIGIOUS LIES, FAMILY AND OR, ANCESTRAL LIES, THE LIES OF OUR FRIENDS AND OTHERS, WE CHOOSE TO SIN AND DIE.

LIFE DO NOT NEED DEATH BUT DEATH NEED LIFE.

WITHOUT LIFE DEATH CANNOT SURVIVE. Yes, your life.

Michelle
August 5, 2021

A real hard cry.
A real hard cry.

To all the great fathers out there big up unnuself.

WICKED BABY MOTHER by Khago

Wow, this song really....

Wow, because this song touch mi heart fi chue.

Some women are like unto Garbage Chute.

It's not about the child but the money they can get out of the man.

Some men truly do not have it financially but if the man is there, support their child with you, teaches that child right from wrong, instill good values into your child, and more good and true things let the man be. Do not chase him out of that child's life.

Yes, some men are worthless.

Some don't care about how their children or child live.

These men, forget them; raise your child good and true as a single mother.

Instill good values in your child.

The struggles will be real. I am speaking from experience.

I do quarrel with my children.

I get attitude, but nothing beats a child that can lift their hand to you and give you a cup of water when you are sick.

Trust me it's not easy for my kids when I am sick. They cannot handle it. At times I don't want to live with them. But wow.

Some of the things some kids do to their parents.

You know what, let me leave it alone because; _SOME USE THEIR BAD EXPERIENCE WITH THE MEN THEY HAVE CHILDREN WITH TO PUNISH THE MAN WITH THEIR CHILDREN._

As an elder, I learnt to not do that therefore, I never did that.

My children lived to know the truth.
My children lived to make their own decision.

If a man is not there they, are truly not there period.

Many men are Sperm Donors because they think children can raise themselves in my view.

It took two to tangle, now a lot of Black Mothers have to bare the burden alone in raising their child and or, children. Sad because; _A LOT OF MEN ARE VALUELESS._

And yes, _IT IS TRULY SAD THAT SOME OF US WOMEN HAVE CHILDREN WITH AND FOR VALUELESS HUMAN BEINGS – NO, DUMPSTERS_, because plenty know not what it means or take to be a father or mother. Thus, men jus use unna fi dumping groune.

Dem come eene like diseases.

All they do is walk from woman to woman and let off their pollution without thinking of the future of that child; thus, many take the blessings of their children from them; thus, the penalty; the charge of adultery, and the penalty of adultery that billions have to; must face in hell.

So yes, some mothers and fathers due literally condemn their children; kids to hell due to their actions; poor choice made in life.

Goodness do pit their child against a good father and mother.

Goodness respects each other.
Goodness is truly not money hungry.
Goodness hath good and true value, and net worth.
Goodness is truly not greedy.

No, I will not go any further, because if I do, I will go off on some disgusting Garbage Chutes that call themselves Mothers and Fathers.

Worthless and Valueless. Therefore, young girls and boys, *NEVER PICK UP GARBAGE AND HAVE CHILDREN FOR THEM.*

AMBITIONLESS DOGS HAVE NO WHERE TO GO IN LIFE.

Thus, many use their vaginas as bus, train, and airport terminals for men.

Hold your head up high and know who to lay with.
Know who to date.

From a girl have no ambition do not stick your Willy in her.

It is not worth it.

It is forbidden for true builders to lay with, marry, and have children with non-builders; yes, users that suck you dry in life.

Sex isn't all because many women and or, many of these young girls done rev out already. Not even hurricane pass by them or through them because even the hurricanes hath life; ambition, and don't want to have anything to do with them.

KNOW:
Their Sin and Sins you do take on if you lay with them. Plus, you take on all the Sins of everyone they've ever laid or lain with.

Some women are crosses. Dem only dey with you fi wey yu ha.

Listen to me keenly. IT IS A CATEGORICAL SIN TO HAVE KIDS WITH THIS WOMAN AND THAT WOMAN. Therefore, do not lay yourself careless.

When you have children for this woman and that woman it is wrong. You are condemning that child to hell. Therefore, know the truth of life.

Kids we say are a blessing yet, AS PARENTS; MANY HAS AND HAVE SEALED THE FATE OF THEIR CHILDREN IN HELL IF THEY HAVE KIDS FOR THIS MAN AND THAT MAN.

Know the truth because, HER SINS; HIS SINS DO FALL ON YOU IF YOU GO FROM WOMAN TO WOMAN AND MAN TO MAN.

1 basis sin is:

1 152 000 000 years in Hell. This penalty do not include the days, months, years, and leap years you've committed that one sin for. Now tell me, do you truly want to spend this much time in hell for 1 sin?

Know the truth and strive not to go to hell.

Polygamy is more than a categorical sin.

Polygamy is NASTY.

Polygamy is NASTY IN THE EYES OF GOD.

Therefore, know the truth of God.
Know the truth of Life.
Know the truth of You.
Know the truth of who you lay with.

Know the truth of who you are going to lay with.
Know the truth all around.

As it is right now, today, and tomorrow; <u>*billions have their*</u> <u>*name in the Book of Death due to lack of knowledge.*</u> Please strive not to go to hell because many things you truly do not know.

Having children should not be about trapping a man or woman.
Having children should not boil down to money; greed.
Having children should be about goodness and truth.

Having children should not be the lack of responsibility as a father and mother.

<u>*Every child have a right in this world. It is us as parents that take*</u> <u>*these rights from our children.*</u>

Some parents teach their child and or, children hate and this should never be. Thus, many parents truly do not know that; <u>*THEIR CHILDREN'S NAME IS WRITTEN IN*</u> <u>*THE BOOK OF DEATH BECAUSE OF THEM.*</u> <u>*Allelujah*</u>

<u>Many kids cannot escape hell because their parents literally made it so.</u>

Do not be like one of these parents.

Set good and true values and moral values for your child and or, children. Yes, some will not adhere to the good and true values you've set. But set them anyway. Your children's sins cannot fall on you if you are a good parent; taught your children right; good and true.

Be there for your child or children.
Do little things with them.

<u>*No child asked to come into this world to be abandoned by mother and father come on now.*</u>

Who the hell wants a part time daddy, or a non-existent daddy?

No, if you know you cannot be a father or mother to a child; have none. Contrary to popular beliefs and what you are taught:

<u>*"NO CHILD IS GUARANTEED TO SAVE YOU IN LIFE BECAUSE NOT ALL CHILDREN ARE A BLESSING UNTO LIFE."*</u>

Yes, go ahead and fume. The truth should not hurt now come on now.

It is a blessed child that thinks of their parents, grand parents, good and true friends, their ancestors in death. Meaning, a blessed child will allocate some of their goodness to those they truly love who have passed away.

No, how many…I was going to say something else, but I will leave it. Now let me ask you this, <u>*and do not include me in the picture.*</u> Take me out of the picture as I am stepping aside briefly while you think.

<u>*"HOW MANY IN HISTORY FROM THE PAST, UNTIL NOW INCLUDING TOMORROW HAS*</u>

71

EVER SAID; GOD; GOOD GOD AND ALLELUJAH, LET SOME OF MY GOOD GO TOWARDS SAVING MY TRUE LOVED ONES, AND THAT PERSON GIVE THE NAMES OF WHO THEIR GOODNESS HERE ON EARTH WHILE LIVING GO TOWARDS SAVING?"

Many say, Jesus died to save them. But let me ask you this. *WAS YOUR NAME INCLUDED ON THE LIST OF SAVED BY JESUS?*

DID JESUS SAY; FATHER GOD, SAVE ELIJAH WAYNE, LET SOME OF MY GOODNESS GO TOWARDS SAVING ELIJAH WAYNE, MARSHALL JEFFERIES, SISTER EDNA THOMAS?

SO, HOW CAN ANYONE SAY JESUS DIED TO SAVE THEM WHEN NONE CAN PRODUCE THE TRUE RECORDS OF JESUS WITH THEIR NAME LISTED ON THAT RECORD?

You cannot live like fools; the uneducated and expect to be saved.

NOW, WHAT BANK ACCOUNT DID JESUS HAVE WITH LOVEY; GOD?

No Lovey truly don't laugh. *BUT WHAT BANK ACCOUNT OR BANK ACCOUNTS DID JESUS HAVE WITH YOU?*

<u>HOW MUCH SAVINGS DID JESUS PUT IN YOU LOVEY COME ON NOW?</u>

So, if Jesus had no Savings or Chequing; no form of investment with you Lovey, how can humans say they are going to die and see you; go to heaven Lovey?

Now the question is, <u>**WHICH HEAVEN?**</u>

<u>HELL IS A HEAVEN FOR SOME BECAUSE THAT'S WHERE BILLIONS ARE GOING TO GO.</u>

As humans, we cannot condemn life and expect to get goodness out of life.

As humans, we cannot do all that is wrong and expect God to give us right; life.

As humans, we cannot have a 0 balance in our Bank Account with God and expect to get life with God once the Spirit shed the Flesh.

As humans, we cannot hate and live for hate and expect to have life with God.

As humans, we cannot live to die and expect to have life with God once the Spirit shed the Flesh.

As humans, we cannot live in vain, live in lies, and expect to have life with God once the Spirit shed the Flesh.

As humans, we cannot believe in lies and accept lies about God and expect God to be pleased with us. God is not pleased therefore, billions did forfeit their life with the lies they accepted about God in the name of Religion.

Therefore, I can categorically tell you without doubt and with the absoluteness of Truth in God and with God that God is not with anyone in any form of Religion.

Everyone under the different banners and names of religion is truly locked out from the Realm of God. Thus, I am telling you truthfully; YOUR NAME IS NOT IN THE BOOK OF LIFE, BUT IN THE BOOK OF DEATH. There are no ands, ifs, or buts about this. This is the absolute truth.

And truly do not believe me.

KNOW.

God do not deal in belief. God; the True and Living God is Knowledge therefore, *KNOW AND KNOW TH TRUTH.*

I am giving you knowledge therefore know; *ALL WHO ARE OF RELIGION IS LOCKED OUT OF THE KINGDOM AND ABODE OF GOD. NOT ONE OF YOU HAVE YOUR NAME IN THE BOOK OF LIFE BUT IN THE BOOK OF DEATH.*

Life is truly not death. Life is good and true life that grows up not down.

74

Therefore, <u>KNOW GOD</u>.

Trust God.
Start saving with God.

Listen, if goodness is not in you, do not rush out and say you are going to do this, this, and this. It will never work.

Absolutely no one can gain goodness in lies come on now.

Michelle
August 5, 2021

A blessed Friday Morning to you all. Don't fry yourself though. Yes, a corny joke so truly forgive me, but a good and blessed morning to you.

I truly hope today is a day filled with happiness, joy, prosperity, all that is good and true you will receive on this day.

I pray that miracles; well, good blessings fall upon you so that you will receive abundantly all the money you need to pay your bills, and have money left over.

I pray all your health troubles and woes will go away permanently never to ever return.

I pray all the issues you are having with your wife, husband, children, enemies, court issues, jail issues, hospital issues and bills, will be resolved in a good and true way that see you find true peace and happiness with the outcome.

I pray God will continually bless all who need God good and true.

I pray God will continually protect all who need God good and true.

I pray God will continually shine his and her light upon you; all who need God good and true.

A Blessed Morning to you all.
Blessed be you good and true.
Blessed be you good and true.

Michelle
August 6, 2021

It is a beautiful day.
The sun is shining.
Weather is just right.
Not too hot.
Not too cold.

I so do not know what is going to happen in Canada and or, somewhere in Canada if not in the world when it comes to the Earth; soil and or, dirt of Earth.

This morning well, not too long ago, I dreamt Mother Ford.

We were in church, and she was dressed in blue I believe.

She had a round white plastic basin like the ones I have in my home. She put dirt in the white plastic basin and shook it then went towards the bathroom. So, I truly do not know if there is going to be an Earthquake in Canada real soon.

I am so not going to worry about it because; DEATH IS PLANTING MORE AND MORE IN CANADA. Canadians have and has lost their way. Therefore, Canada is going to pay and pay dearly for their continued disobedience. So yes, DEATH IS PREPARING TO DEVASTATE CANADA.

Did I dream about my seeds?

Yes

They did not bud, were not growing and did not grow. One seed was split; did not look good.

So yes, there is something wrong with the seeds I planted for God. And I know this because my cherry seeds have not budded. Yes, disappointing on my part but this is my life.

My hands are not blessed in that way, and this is truly a bummer for me.

Maybe one day I will plant in a different land and a tree will grow. So, no, I should not expect growth with me and God in Canada seed wise because my true and good heart is truly not with this land; Canada, or any North American Land for that matter.

Life is good but sometimes life do not turn out the way we expect it to.

I am truly happy I planted the seeds I needed for God. I just hope now God find the true peace and happiness he and or, she requires to continue to live and grow good and true continually all the time. So, yes, Lovey and God I bless you good and true, and hope that we continue to grow in true goodness and truth all the time.

So, a Blessed Morning to you Lovey.

I pray all you required of me was and is pleasing to you.

I pray that all your aches and pain are washed away permanently to never ever return unto you.

I pray sincerely that you find all the goodness and truth you need in life.

I pray true peace and true happiness for you.

I pray your life grow good and true in value.
Worth
Strength
True love
And more good and true things.

I pray your days are clear, clean, filled with abundance of goodness and truth.

I pray you continually stay safe, whole, pure, truly loving.

I pray you continually live good and true without end.

I pray you find all you need in life good and true.

Lovey, a Blessed Morning to you.
A Blessed Morning to you.

May no sickness come your way.

May all your fruit baskets be always full.

May the clean and clear waters of life continually find you, bless you, surround you, fill you with joy and happiness good and true.

May all the goodness you require in life come to fruition.

May all the goodness you require in life truly bless you good and true.

A Blessed Morning to you Lovey.
A Blessed Morning.

May you continually be encouraged to do all that is right and true.

On this day and forever ever, let me continue to encourage you, be there for you, continue to be your good and true friend, even if I cuss you out on some days.

Stay true.

True love always and never ending.

Michelle
August 2021

Wow

It's evening time and I am just finding out something.

You know, as parents you can do all you can to raise your children the right way, but some truly do not take telling or even care for the right way in life.

Family
Children

That's all I got to say because I am finding out the hard way that; *LIFE MEANS NOTHING TO MANY IN THE YOUNGER GENERATION.*

Life is but a bleeping game.

I so can't live like this because my expectations of life is not the same as other people. It seems as if evil is winning and good is losing; failing.

I can't blame God for this because; *HUMANS DO HAVE A CHOICE TO DO WRONG OR RIGHT.* What is right for me is truly not right for others. Therefore, what is right for me is truly not what's right for my daughter.

I am so going to say, she's just a *TOTAL DISAPPOINTMENT IN LIFE, AND IN MY LIFE RIGHT NOW.*

And I am going to leave things as is because we truly do not get along.

My morals and moral values are truly not hers.
My life's worth and life values are truly not hers.

My Sins are not her Sins, and her Sins are not my Sins.

Right now, I have to look at myself and ask; *WHAT THE HELL IS WRONG WITH THE YOUNGER GENERATION OF BLACK MALES AND FEMALES?*

WHERE THE HELL DID BLACK VALUES EVAPORATE TO?

WHEN DID WE LOSE SIGHT OF US AND OUR BLACK VALUES, GOD, RIGHTS, MORALS, MORAL VALUES, AND MORE?

Yes, I know a stupid question on my part, but then; I know the truth because; *BLACK PEOPLE INCLUDING AFRICANS TRULY DO NOT KNOW WHAT IT IS TO BE TRULY BLACK PERIOD.*

No Lovey. I am literally loathing life here on Earth.

Life here on Earth stinks; is worse than shit to how people live, have no respect for each other, cannot value their life, or the life of others.

No, what my daughter did.

Truly there is absolutely no forgiveness in my book for that. Worthless on her part.

Valueless on her part.

Therefore, I ask Lovey. *IS NOTHING SACRED ANYMORE HERE ON EARTH?*

Yes, another stupid question on my part. From the way humans cast you, believe in crap of shit about you, nothing including You is Sacred anymore Lovey.

Humans live for evil.
Bask in evil.
Trend in evil.
Marry in evil.
Procreate in evil.
Die in evil, and more.

No Lovey, this isn't the way therefore, *I MICHELLE JEAN IS BOYCOTTING LIFE HERE ON EARTH.*

I BOYCOTT LIFE – THE EVIL WAY OF LIFE HERE ON EARTH.

I TRULY CANNOT STAND LIVING HERE ON EARTH ANYMORE.

NO, LOVEY, I CANNOT FORGIVE YOU FOR THIS.

I CANNOT FORGIVE YOU FOR NOT SEPARATING GOOD FROM EVIL HERE ON EARTH.

I made my choice for good and true life, and you've deserted me when it comes to life; a good and true life here on Earth therefore, I have to boycott life here on Earth with You and Mother Earth because, *neither of you truly care about my life, my true well being, and more.*

Yes, what I am finding out truly hurt me because you both know how much I value Life; my life and the life of others; to now find out this!!!!

No, what is the point of me begging for the good and true and truly trying to be good when we are surrounded by all that is truly wicked and evil?

What is the point of begging you for good and true life for me here on Earth, and all around me is failure?

Humans lack value, moral values, and more.

So, yes, I am truly disappointed in life because life here on Earth do not have to be this way; so evil, vile, malicious, lying, deceiving, unclean, ugly, and more disgusting, and disappointing things.

No Lovey. How do I look at You and Mother Earth and value the both of you now?

Yes, from what I wrote this morning until now is unbelievable on my part. I still do truly love You and Mother Earth, but my daughter truly disappointed me.

You know what Lovey. *IT'S HER LIFE AND SIN.*

SHE HAS TO; MUST ACCOUNT FOR IT.

Wow, because.......let it go Michelle, let it go.

You are disappointed but let your good and true life reign.

Add value to your life now come on now.
Continue to stay strong.

Continue to do that which is right for you.
Continue to build you despite your hurt and pain.

Continue to do the good that you can.
Stay strong in God and Mother Earth.
Stay strong Physically.
Stay strong Spiritually.

You know hell.
You know the cost of each sin.

You know what your daughter and others have to face in hell.

You cannot beg for your disobedient children anymore.

You have to learn to let go.

You know the life history and bloodline of her father's side of the family.

You know the life history and bloodline of your father's and mother's side of your family. Stay strong and live up. Never live down because good and true life goes up.

Encourage yourself now.
Encourage you.

Be the good and true you you need to be for you and Lovey including, Mother Earth and your good and true guides that direct you from time to time.

Yes, I have to stay encouraged because if I don't, I will lose my way.

I have to stay focused because if my anger set in right now, Hell would literally freeze over.

I have to stay focused because if my anger set in right now. Nothing will be left standing in my apartment.

Let it be.
Let it go.

Stay focused on life.
Stay focused on God.

Keep trying Michelle.

Keep trying.

This is just another test.
Another trial.
Another tribulation.

Don't think of your daughter and her actions.

Walk it off.

Go take Queenie for a walk because she needs to go out.

Go with God right and true.

Remember, you are getting better.
You washed yesterday and today.

You went out with your sons.

Despite your son's car breaking down and needing repairs that is going to cost him to fix. You had a beautiful day with your sons.

Yes, your last child has improved with his attitude tremendously.

Keep praying.
Keep living.

Keep breathing slowly and true.

Keep being the good and true you, you need to be.

Live up
Live up
God is able
God is with you

God is guiding you
God is keeping you
God is securing you

Keep trying

Keep going to God with everything.
Keep God handy all the time with you.

Let God continue to be your speed dial.

Go too person.
Radio station.
All

God is able.
God is able.
God is able.

God will work things out right and just for you.

God will forever keep you secure.

Let your daughter be.
Let her be.
Let her be.

Because you know what Michelle.

God is there for you.
God is your able.
God is your right.
God is your joy.

Stand firm.
Stand still.
Stand true and right with God.

Allelujah

Thank you, God and Lovey.
Truly thank you.

I have to stand.
I am standing with you good and true.

I am not broken.
I am right.
I am right.
Allelujah.
Wow

Thank you Lovey
Truly thank you Lovey.

Michelle
August 6, 2021

I cannot give up despite me wanting to.

Yes, life I am loathing right now, but I have to hold on. A better life is coming for me, I know this Lovey because I truly trust you.

I have to continue to trust you despite my disappointment and anger.

Yes, I am calm now.

I have to stay calm and not let my anger get the best of me anymore.

The younger generation is truly different; therefore, all have their own cross and burden that they must carry and bare.

I guess in many ways Lovey, we are not so different. Some of us as parents are trying to teach our children right but they don't take your teaching due to them, friends; the different environment they circulate in friendship wise, what they see others do, and more.

With us as humans and You Lovey. How many adhere to the truth of life?

Are we not influenced by outside influences like the church; what the clergies of the different religions tell us who you are, what you're all about based on lies; the lies they tell and preach?

Are Generational Lies not the same?

What we were taught to be the truth hence, lies are handed down from generation to generation therefore, lies do not stop. Thus, the Sins of every human here on Earth, and in the Spiritual Realm.

Lies do carry forward hence:
Generational Lies
Family Lies
Historical Lies
Religious Lies
Judicial Lies
Political Lies
Educational Lies
Corporate Lies
Scientific Lies
And more.

In all you've tried with us as humans Lovey; have you not failed Lovey?

Have I not failed?

Have I not failed when it comes to some of my children?

Our minds are not the same therefore, people form their own views, are influenced and brainwashed by others. Negativity is the norm here on Earth Lovey and this is truly sad.

What is right for us Lovey is truly not right for others. Yes, you want to save humanity, but humanity has and have proven time and time again that; *they truly do not want to be saved.* Thus, life has and have become dirty; unclean for billions. These billions you have to leave alone because life hath no merit to them; these billions.

90

What is truly sadder is that; humans want to be saved from Hell yet, refuse to give up their wrong ways here on Earth.

Yes, many cannot live for life or by life.

You know what Lovey, I truly do not want or need to justify humans because, I am disappointed in the way billions have turned out.

Billions live for Death and this is their good and true will, and I have to leave these people alone. You too Lovey have to leave these people alone.

Listen, Lovey, _the Book of Life with you right now. Just close it._

Complete this book and be truly satisfied with the Names that are written in your good and true book. Also, if it is just and fair; right and good, please put my name, the name of my mother, all my saved, your saved, and the saved of the saved and truly trying to be good including, the truly trying to be good beside our; well, your good and true name.

Lovey, can life get more disheartening?

No, we have to complete life here on Earth. Therefore, let things be done now.

The lies and life of the wicked and evil cannot extend or go beyond 2032. It's time You Lovey, and Mother Earth truly do right by life for the good and true here on Earth.

Yes, I said I do not want to plea for humans anymore, but in good and true truth, I cannot give up on the good and true and truly trying to be good here on Earth.

91

Aye Lovey, let me put my head on your shoulder.
Let me rest a little while with you because I truly need you.

It's time we move out of the domain and domains of wicked and evil humans; people.

Aye, the creation of a new Earth is there, but I did not want the power to do so.

Yes, Lovey that unlimited power to create a new Earth is there, but it would not be fair and just due to my anger. I truly want and need to create void of all Negative Forces, void of all Evil, void of all Negative Energy; all that is wicked and evil including, void of all negative and evil humans and spirit.

Aye Lovey, I truly need to increase my knowledge.

So much I need, but limited in acquiring my need and true needs.

It's not 11pm yet but I am going to go to my bed. I need to relax, sleep, and not think of all that is happening in my household, around the globe; world, in my family, with humans, the carnage on land globally, and more.

Lovey, you and Mother Earth truly have a blessed night.

Lovey, if it's possible, You and Mother Earth truly pray good and true for me as well as, shower your good and true blessing on me. I need it right now because life here on Earth is truly not getting better. And yes, I truly know I don't have to worry about life because I am saved and safe with You and Mother Earth.

Lovey, why can't humans see the preciousness of life?

Why can't humans see You and Mother Earth good and true?

No Lovey, why did you have to be separated from Earth?

It's like single parenthood with You and Mother Earth?

No Lovey and Mother Earth. Being a single parent sucks.

Why Single Parenthood Lovey and Mother Earth?

No Lovey and Mother Earth, where is a good and true place here on Earth for us to live and communicate with each other?

It's hard. It's like Queenie and how she tries to communicate with me via her language.

You know she is trying to talk but she can only speak in the language of dogs and not humans.

Yes, she comprehends certain things in human language, but the communication barrier is still there because she cannot articulate her words in human form for me to comprehend her.

In the afternoon when I was washing my bra and socks, she hurried into the washroom where I was. I do not know why she did that as if spooked and looking for something and or, someone around me. Weird because she has her different ways of protecting me I guess.

Yes, I know the evil hence....leave it alone Michelle. Leave it alone because you see beyond many things, and the darkness that lurks within hence your death; the dead that surrounds you from time to time protecting you.

So, truly thank you Lovey and Mother Earth for truly being you good and true.

Michelle
August 6, 2021

I truly need to change my glasses.

Good morning sunshine, it's a beautiful day.

It's August 8, 2021 and I am so not going to worry about the day.

Life is good.
Life is how we make it.

Had a fantastic day yesterday.

It was my daughter's Earth Day. Well, the day she fully took her place here on Earth on her own; well, for the first time not being in my tummy.

Just being around young people, I have to say I am a true dinosaur. Young kids are innovative, and many truly know what they want and need in life. Therefore, as parents, we have to; must let our children follow their dream as well as, live their dream.

God is too from the way I see things. Listen, in life there is......

No, <u>as parents we have to allow our children to choose their own path in life.</u> Our children cannot live our life for us because we are living our life. They; our children have to live their own life the way they see and deem fit.

As parents we have to realize, kids need to have fun.
They need to socialize.
They need their own balance in their life.
They need to make their own decisions in their life.
They need to think for self.
They need good and true encouragement.

As parents we can't be down their throats all the time.

95

We cannot choice our children's life path for them in life. Our children have to; must do this all on their own.

I am so not a people person, but I will tell my children, have fun in life, save for the future, make wise decisions from now and live.

Listen fully and truly.

<u>LIVING CLEAN HATH NO BOUNDARIES TO CLEANLINESS.</u>

<u>LIVING CLEAN TRULY DO NOT MEAN YOU CANNOT HAVE FUN IN LIFE.</u>

<u>KNOWING GOD AND LIVING WITH GOD DO NOT MEAN YOU CANNOT HAVE FUN IN LIFE.</u>

<u>LISTEN, GOD IS NOT CHRISTIAN, MUSLIM, ORTHODOX, PROTESTANT, WHATEVER YOU NAME HIM RELIGIOUSLY, GOD IS TRULY NOT THAT ENTITY; BEING; LIFE, LIFE SOURCE, AND MORE.</u>

<u>All God requires is for us to live good, true, clean, truly loving, kind, truly caring, and more good and true things.</u>

I vent a lot in these books yes, but God should always be your good and true source in life and of life.

Living clean does not mean you cannot go to the club if clubbing is your scene. However, if you go to a club do not go to pick up your next trick, fix, woman, or man.

Dance and have fun, eat and drink but if you drink know your limit. Do not drink to get drunk or make a fool of yourself.

If you have a wife or mate at home, respect the person you left at home.

Whatever your good and true fun is; whether it be snow boarding, hiking, biking, have true and clean fun doing you.

Yes, seeing the younger generation having fun, I realize you cannot cage them; the younger generation. You cannot force values; your values on anyone including your children; they will rebel. Let your child and or, children have fun by directing them in the right direction.

Many of us as Black People, use religion to brainwash, cage, manipulate, and take away the fun years and life of our children, and we can no longer do that as parents.

CAGING OUR CHILDREN IN CAGES ESPECIALLY RELIGIOUS CAGES IS WRONG.

THE BIBLE IS NOT RIGHT FOR ANYONE THEREFORE, WE NEED TO FIND WHAT IS RIGHT AND TRUE IN LIFE, AND LIVE BY OUR GOOD AND TRUE TRUTHS AND VALUES. What we value in life is not necessarily what our children value in life.

What I know to be the true is not the truth they; our children are taught in school.

What I know to be the truth is not what the clergies of the church teach our children to be the truth.

What I know to be the truth is not what is mandated by Society or the different Governments of the Globe.

What I know to be the truth is not what is mandated by the different Corporations of the Globe.

What I know to be the truth is not what is mandated by the different Armies and Cultures of the Globe, and more.

GOD DO NOT CAGE HUMANS, NO, I THINK GOD CAGES PEOPLE. But my view is wrong. God's protection is not caging anyone. God's protection is protecting you physically and spiritually.

Our children are growing. It's time we grow them right by directing them good and true; right.

It's time we as parents, STOP CLASHING WITH OUR CHILDREN.

It's time as parents, WE BEGIN TO LISTEN TO OUR CHILDREN.

SEE OUR CHILDREN'S VIEW(S).
THINK ABOUT THEIR VIEWS.

It's time as parents, WE START KNOWING OUR CHILDREN.

So yes, with what my daughter did, I said I cannot forgive her, but after yesterday and talking to some of the young crowd, I have to forgive her because; MY DAUGHTER'S WAY OF THINKING IS TRULY NOT MY WAY OF THINKING.

EVERY CHILD HAVE TO COME INTO THEIR OWN LIFE WISE.

EVERY CHILD HAVE TO MAKE THEIR OWN DECISIONS WHEN THEY GET TO A CERTAIN AGE.

As parents, WE NEED TO START ENCOURAGING OUR CHILDREN.

Yes, as parents we were raised differently, but as time moves forward, we as parents have to learn and know that it is not that time is changing, <u>**BUT THE MINDSET OF OUR CHILDREN ARE CHANGING. DIFFERENT THINGS INFLUENCE THEM DIFFERENTLY IN LIFE.**</u>

<u>DIFFERENT FRIENDS AND THE DIFFERENT CULTURES OF THE DIFFERENT HUMANS DO INFLUENCE OUR CHILDREN DUE TO THE FRIENDS; THE COMPANY THEY KEEP.</u>

God is not racist. Humans are.

As long as you are clean, he or she is clean, good, true, then God have and has no problem with whom you choose in life. God will give his or her approval.

Yes, BABYLONIANS WE ARE FORBIDDEN TO LAY WITH. But with God this has absolutely nothing to do with race or colour. THIS HAS ALL TO DO WITH LIFE; <u>THE DIFFERENT GODS BABYLONIANS PRAISE AND WORSHIP THEREFORE, THE CHILDREN OF BABYLON IS TRULY NOT A PART OF THE LIFE OF GOD DUE TO DEATH; THEIR GOD AND GODS.</u>

Michelle
August 2021

Whether you like what I wrote about:

THE FLAGS OF DEATH

CROSSES OF DEATH

COUNTRIES OF DEATH IN LIFE AFTER DEATH.

This is truly up to you. I am not here to debate with you or anyone about these truths. It is us as humans that buy into lies and when the truth comes along you deny it.

Keep denying the truth because I know for a fact without doubt that lies cannot save you, and will never ever save you.

You cannot accept lies and think God will be please with you, and I keep telling you this.

GOD IS NOT PLEASED WITH HUMANS. *Therefore, GOD DO NOT INTERFERE WITH THE CHOICE AND CHOICES BILLIONS OF YOU MAKE IN LIFE WELL, HERE ON EARTH.*

After the spirit shed the flesh, if your name in not written in the Book of Life you cannot be saved.

I truly do not care if your God and Saviour is Jesus, YOU CANNOT AND WILL NEVER EVER GO UP TO SEE LOVEY; GOD.

God is not belief.

GOD IS KNOWLEDGE; WISDOM.

If you have not knowledge of the truth, how can you know?

There is Life and there is Death. **AFTER THE SHEDDING OF FLESH IS WHERE ALL IS FINALIZED.**

Here on Earth, you either have Life or you have Death.

YOU CANNOT HAVE BOTH ONCE THE SPIRIT SHED THE FLESH.

Here on Earth, we live amongst the Children and People of Life as well as, live amongst the Children and People of Death. This can no longer be. Positive changes must come to Earth and stay on Earth. The Time of Death and or, Satan is up. I refuse to extend the Life of Death and or, Satan and their wicked and evil own here on Earth.

Thus, Mother Earth have to; must do her part in evicting the wicked and evil from in her. Therefore, Good must separate self from all facets of Evil here on Earth.

Thus, as evil cannot enter the domain of God in the Spiritual Realm, evil cannot and must never ever enter the Domain of Earth ever again. There has to be a final stop to evil. Life can no longer be amongst the wicked and evil. The Children and People of Death must go with Death literally. No home must ever be found on or in Mother Earth for them; the Children and People of Death including Death come on now.

The choice to live and the choice to die is truly not up to God or Death. It is up to every human whether living or dead.

102

The choice we make is either final with Death or Final with Life; God. Therefore, know the choice you made.

How do you know this you may ask?

You know this through and or, by your sins and the different sins you commit; do.

Sins like:
Cheating which is adultery and polygamy.
Lies you tell daily.
Going to church.

No take going to church out. Death owns you when you go to church because it is Death you are worshipping and praising.

Marriage upon marriage without being properly divorced.
Self hate and the hating of others.
Strife you make and commit with others.

The Armies of Death you belong to.

No take out the Armies of Death you belong to. Death owns you thus, you have willingly and knowingly broken the "thou shalt not kill" law. Thus, disobedience is automatic death. _You have your go straight to hell card._

Theft, and more. Therefore, you get the picture clearly.

And I am so going to leave things here until later and or, another day.

Michelle
August 11, 2021

It's after 1pm and I've not had breakfast. Did not want to eat so I had coffee.

I am getting a bit hungry, and I am going to make something to eat as I am toggling between two books.

Trying to edit LIFE AFTER DEATH on the computer.

My Selenite Crystal that I had on my bed fell off the bed.

So, my dream about it breaking came true. It broke and you could see the breakage, and I just popped it and threw it in the garbage.

I still have my big one, but I am going to leave that one alone because it has cracks.

All has and have served their purpose and now it's time for me to move on with my journey.

I am connecting to a higher source, and this is truly good for me.

I am also trying to connect to the inner me, but it is a long and difficult process, but I am on the right track.

My Mind though is a pain in the butt because it won't let up on the chatter. So, yes, the Mind do hinder your Spiritual Progress.

Michelle
August 11, 2021

BOOKS WRITTEN BY MICHELLE JEAN 2021

MY TALK JANUARY 2021

MY TALK JANUARY 2021 – BOOK TWO

MINI BOOK

JUST TALKING – THINKING

A LITTLE TALK WITH MOTHER EARTH

I NEED ANSWERS GOD

POETRY MY WAY

THE MIND AND SPIRITUALITY

I NEED ANSWERS GOD – PART TWO

MY NIGHTS

I NEED ANSWERS GOD – PART THREE

GOD IS GOOD

WHAT ABOUT US

WOW WHAT

AFRICAN – BLACK PEOPLE CUSS OUT

THE FIFTH WAVE – BLACK PEOPLE WARNING

FINAL CALL

JUST MY TALK 2021

THE TRAP

CHANGES

RACIST OR NOT

GIVE ME A REASON – SPIRITUAL CLEANSING

LIFE AFTER DEATH

COMING SOON

MOVING UP – MY HEART TO HEART WITH LOVEY – GOD 2021

DAY BY DAY

* 1 6 0 7 5 1 7 3 1 *1